D1237438

ARABIAN HORSES

by Cari Meister

AMICUS | AMICUS INK

Amicus High Interest and Amicus Ink are published by Amicus
P.O. Box 1329, Mankato, MN 56002
www.amicuspublishing.us

Library of Congress Cataloging-in-Publication Data
Names: Meister, Cari, author.
Title: Arabian horses / by Cari Meister.
Description: Mankato, Minnesota : Amicus, [2019] | Series: Favorite horse breeds | Includes index.
Identifiers: LCCN 2017036883 (print) | LCCN 2017048296 (ebook) | ISBN 9781681515069 (pdf) | ISBN 9781681514246 (library bound) | ISBN 9781681523446
Subjects: LCSH: Arabian horse--Juvenile literature.
Classification: LCC SF293.A8 (ebook) | LCC SF293.A8 M45 2019 (print) | DDC 636.1/12--dc23
LC record available at https://lccn.loc.gov/2017036883

Photo Credits: Kwadrat70/Dreamstime cover; Olga_i/Shutterstock 2, 22; Jeff Vanuga/Getty 5; Hussain Nalwala/Shutterstock 6-7; Thaliastock/Mary Evans 8-9; Somogyvari/Getty 10-11; rokopix/Shutterstock 12-13; Birgid Allig/Getty 14-15; Makarova Viktoria/Shutterstock 17; Kerrick/Getty 18-19; Maria itina/Getty 20-21

Editor: Wendy Dieker
Designer: Veronica Scott
Photo Researcher: Holly Young

Printed in China

HC 10 9 8 7 6 5 4 3 2 1
PB 10 9 8 7 6 5 4 3 2 1

TABLE OF CONTENTS

A LONG RACE

A horse jumps over a log. He runs by the woods. He rests. He runs more. He goes 50 miles (80.5 km). It is an **endurance race**. This horse can go and go! He is an Arabian horse.

Did You Know?

Any horse can run in an endurance race. But Arabians win endurance races more often than any other breed.

4

BUILT FOR A LONG RUN

An Arabian's light body helps it run a long time. It also has big **nostrils** that take in lots of air. Its legs are thick and strong.

DESERT HORSES

The Arabian horse was bred in
the Middle East about 4,000
years ago. People in this desert
region needed hardy horses.

PRIZED HORSES

People brought Arabians around the world. They became prized horses everywhere. Most horse **breeds** today have a bit of Arabian in them.

A GRACEFUL TROT

It is easy to spot an Arabian horse. It runs with its head and tail up. It is very graceful. It seems to float in the air when it is trotting.

ELEGANT POSTURE

An Arabian's tail has two fewer bones than other horses have. This horse has one fewer pair of ribs. Its back is shorter as well. This gives the horse an elegant **posture**.

SUN PROTECTION

Arabian horses have black skin. It helps protect them from the sun. Their coats can be one of five colors. They are chestnut, gray, black, bay, or **rabicano**. A rabicano horse has white flecks.

FOALS

Arabian **mares** are pregnant with a **foal** for 11 months. Most foals are born at night. They stand almost right away. They drink milk. They grow fast!

Did You Know?

An Arabian horse can live to be 25 to 30 years old.

KIND AND GENTLE

Arabian horses are kind. They want to please. They are gentle. They like to be around people. They are loyal. They want to be your friend for life.

HOW DO YOU KNOW IT'S AN ARABIAN HORSE?

small, curved ears

dished face

tail held high

short back

14 to 15 hands

WORDS TO KNOW

breed – a kind of horse that has a certain set of characteristics and has ancestors of the same breed.

endurance race – a horseback race that covers a long distance; many endurance races are 50 miles (80.5 km) long.

foal – a baby horse.

mare – a female horse.

nostril – an opening of the nose that allows animals to breathe in and out.

posture – the shape and position of an animal's body.

rabicano – having a coat of a dark color flecked with white hairs; the white flecking is often uneven and has more white on certain parts of the body.

LEARN MORE

Books

Dell, Pamela. *Arabians*. North Mankato, Minn.: Child's World, 2014.

Kolpin, Molly. *Favorite Horses: Breeds Girls Love*. North Mankato, Minn.: Capstone, 2015.

Websites

ArabianHorses.org – Fun Stuff
https://www.arabianhorses.org/youth/fun-stuff/

Horse Channel – Arabian Horses
http://www.horsechannel.com/horse-breeds/profiles/
arabian-horse-breed.aspx

INDEX